GERALDINE McCAUGHREAN

PIONEERS
~at~
PIANO RIDGE

Illustrated by
Chris Molan

OXFORD
UNIVERSITY PRESS

OXFORD
UNIVERSITY PRESS

Great Clarendon Street, Oxford OX2 6DP

Oxford University Press is a department of the University of Oxford.
It furthers the University's objective of excellence in research, scholarship,
and education by publishing worldwide in

Oxford New York

Athens Auckland Bangkok Bogotá Buenos Aires Calcutta
Cape Town Chennai Dar es Salaam Delhi Florence Hong Kong Istanbul
Karachi Kuala Lumpur Madrid Melbourne Mexico City Mumbai
Nairobi Paris São Paulo Shanghai Singapore Taipei Tokyo Toronto Warsaw

and associated companies in Berlin Ibadan

Oxford is a trade mark of Oxford University Press
in the UK and in certain other countries

Text © Geraldine McCaughrean 2001
The moral rights of the author have been asserted
Database right Oxford University Press (maker)
First published 2001

British Library Cataloguing in Publication Data
Data available

ISBN 0 19 915954 8

Printed in Hong Kong

Available in packs

Year 4 / Primary 5 Pack of Six (one of each book) ISBN 0 19 915955 6
Year 4 / Primary 5 Class Pack (six of each book) ISBN 0 19 915956 4

for Natasha H

Contents

1

Trail Blazers

My Pa says we are the heroes of the nation. He says we are pioneers, opening up America for those who come after. He says we're blazing a trail across the wilderness, to create a Land of Milk and Honey.

My Pa builds sawmills. All the time I was growing up in the East, in the big city, he was away for months and months working. So there was just Ma and little Marty and me. I went to school just down the road and Marty (being so little) just cried or slept. He doesn't seem to sleep so much these days. "Marty is bigger now," said Ma one day. "Big enough to travel." So now everything is going to be different. Now we are all travelling Out West to live with Pa. And Pa is going to stop building sawmills and run one instead. We are going to build a house and keep animals and ride to school in a buggy, to a town called Cedar Falls.

Cedar Falls isn't built yet, of course. I sure hope they build the schoolhouse last, so I can stay home for years and look after those animals.

My name is Perry, by the way. It means 'fairy' but don't let that put you off. I'm nine and big for my age, and I never get ill. Ma says, "Perry, you could eat a moose for dinner and still be hungry by suppertime."

Maybe she's right. I never saw a moose.

2
Going West

I've never been so scared. I've never
been so tired. I've never been so hungry.
Moving Out West was horrible. For one
thing, we left behind half the furniture.

"What about the piano?" I said,
when no one loaded it into the wagon.

"Perry, it's too heavy," said Ma, "and
we won't have a house to live in, first
off, and you can't keep a piano in a
tent."

So why did I have all those lessons, that's what I want to know? Maybe people Out West never have pianos. Maybe they don't have any music at all! What a thought! Suppose they don't know the words to any songs? Maybe they have to just hum and la-la.

Ma says we might send for the piano when the house is ready: that's what people do. Does that mean there are whole wagon trains full of big, old lonely pianos going Out West to find their owners?

That's how we got here. We joined a wagon train heading West, and we travelled with it for weeks and weeks and weeks. Ma thought the worst thing was the dust: dust in the bedrolls, dust in the food, dust on our toys, dust inside our clothes. But the dust wasn't the worst.

Marty thought the worst was the shaking and rattling. The wagons banged over the ground as if they had square wheels. It nearly shook the teeth out of our heads. It nearly broke our bones. There were hills so steep the horses couldn't pull the wagons, so we had to help by pushing. One wagon slid over the edge of a ravine into a river, and cribs and clothes and food went washing away down river. But the

shaking wasn't the worst.

I thought the heat was worse. It made your eyes see orange-and-black patches. It made your clothes stick to you like wet bandages. It made your head ache and your lips crack. It made our skin turn brown. But the heat wasn't the worst.

Worst was the sickness.

One of the children in the other

wagons must have had measles when we set off. It quickly spread from wagon to wagon. Men got it, mothers got it, the ramrods got it. Marty and I got it. There were no doctors, and there was no medicine. Back East we could have gone down the road to buy medicine. Back East the doctor would have called. Back East, Ma would have drawn the curtains, tiptoed softly over the carpet and shut the door quietly behind her.

We just had to go on travelling: shake-shake-rattle, orange-and-black patches, no doctor, and the dust sticking to our spots. I thought I would die.

Some of the old people did.

I was never sick Back East. What if everyone gets ill Out West? What if all the doctors are too sensible to move there?

Pa says we didn't meet with the

worst. He says the worst thing would have been savages – an injun attack. He says that injuns steal women and children and keep them prisoners for the rest of their lives.

"What do they do with the men?" I wanted to know.

"Don't ask," said Pa darkly.

Oh Lor'! What if Ma and Pa die of measles Out West? Or get killed by savages, and Marty and I have to live together all on our own in a tent at Cedar Falls? I wish we were Back East. Back home.

3
Piano Ridge

Piano Ridge is the most beautiful place
in the world. There are rivers
everywhere, and so many trees that the
mountains seem to be wearing green fur
coats. The woods are measle-speckled
with berries. In the mornings, there are
deer standing outside the tent, staring
and flicking their ears.

We are living in two tents – one for Ma and Pa, one for Marty and me – right next to a bend in the river. One day our house will stand here, the river in front and the hills behind. Pa has already cut the logs he needs to build it.

His sawmill is on the other side of a hill we call Piano Ridge. It's true, it is shaped like a piano (though you would need giant fingers to play it). It doesn't make me miss my piano lessons, but it does remind me of Ma playing the piano in the evenings, back home. I miss that terribly.

Sometimes the silence here is too big for me.

The logs come floating down river from the mill like crocodiles – hundreds and hundreds of huge brown crocodiles. We can see the smoke from the fire where they burn all the twigs and leaves trimmed off the logs. Most of the timber will be used to build the new town. Pa makes railway sleepers too, for the railroad company. One day, the railroad will come through Cedar Falls. So maybe our piano can travel by train instead. I think it would prefer that.

4

The Trout Pool

Pa has been promising for weeks to take me fishing. At long last he did. We could not fish in the big river, of course. All those logs have scared off the fish. No, we followed a brook that runs into the big river, and climbed upstream along its banks to a place so wild that it doesn't even have a name yet.

"Are you sure there aren't any

savages in the forest?" Ma said before we left home. "Or dangerous beasts?"

"I'm sure," said Pa. But he took his gun just in case.

Pa always keeps his gun close to hand. He says that pioneers have to be on their guard night and day, because injuns are so sneaky and cruel. He says they don't believe in God and that's what makes them wicked. He says the Government wants settlers like us, because we will make the country a civilized, Christian place. When I have nightmares about injuns coming out of the forests, Pa shows me his gun and promises, "I'll shoot any savage who dares to set foot on our land!" He is very brave, my Pa.

Between two noisy, rushing stretches of stream, we found a big, smooth pool as deep as doom, but clear all the way to the bottom. And there were so many trout! They flittered about like ghosts on Hallowe'en. And one of them was a real monster of a fish!

"I'm taking that one home to Ma!" I said, "And that's a promise!" So we put bread on our hooks and fished all morning. It didn't do us any good. I blame Marty. He was just *awful*. I knew we should have left him back at the tents, with Ma. He would *not* keep quiet. He would *not* keep still. He kept spooking the fish with his shouting and running about.

I got so wild that I said to Pa, "Can't you tie him down or something?"

Marty heard me and stuck out his tongue. Then he picked up a big stone and threw it into the pool: SPLASH!

Down went the fish – away into the weed and crevices at the bottom of the pool.

Well, that made Pa as wild as I was, and he took Marty by the ear and marched him downstream to another pool, and told him not to come back our way until he was called.

Pa and I held very, very still.
Gradually, one by one, the fish
came out again. Last of all came
my big trout – big as a marrow,
I swear! I put more bread on
my hook and
let it down
slowly,
slowly,
slowly…
Then
there
was this
almighty
splash and,
seconds later, a blood-
curdling yell. Marty had fallen
in! We dropped our rods and
ran.

Marty was floundering
around, up to his waist in

water, crying fit to bust. "A redskin pushed me in! A redskin pushed me in!" he hollered.

"Little liar," I said.

Pa went in and hauled him out and told him he was never to tell fibs or mess about near water again. But the damage was already done. By the time we got back to the upper pool, my fishing rod had floated right out from the bank, and its line was all tangled up with a mat of broken twigs in the middle. He always ruins everything, Marty.

Pa told me to take him straight home to Ma.

"I'll catch you up," he said. I was tempted to take Marty to some high cliff and drop him off, but then we heard this huge bang. It echoed all through the woods. Pa came striding after us. And there was my trout – the monster one –

hanging from his fist! "Well, a promise is a promise!" he said laughing.

"How did you do it, Pa?" I asked, and he patted his rifle-butt and winked.

I thought we could eat my trout for dinner, but dinner was already cooked by the time we got home. So I filled a bucket at the river and put the trout in it to keep it fresh overnight.

"Which one of you caught this fine fish?" asked Ma when I presented it to her.

"I did!" I said.

"Little liar," said Marty.

5

The Intruder

Ma told me the fish had to stay outside the tent that night, in case it began to smell. But while I was lying in bed, I kept thinking about it, wondering how it would taste next day, and who would get the slice with the bullet in it.

"Why don't you believe me? An injun pushed me in! He did! He really did!" said Marty for the fiftieth time.

"Little liar," I said for the fiftieth time.

Then I got to thinking. What if some real live injun sneaked out of the woods and stole my trout in the night? Just suppose! So I got up and fetched the bucket inside. No one saw me. The other tent was lamp-lit, but there were no shadows inside. Ma and Pa had gone for a walk in the moonlight, as usual. The grass was cold and dew-wet under my feet. Only the trout looked up at me with silver eyes. Ma was right: it did smell a bit more than it had when we put it in the bucket.

Suddenly, something rustled in the bushes down by the river. Well, you never saw anyone move as fast as I did then. I ran back to my tent as quick as any jackrabbit, and jumped into my bedroll and pulled the covers over my head.

It was cosy in there. I

told myself I was being a silly coward. It was probably just a beaver or a hedgehog. Fancy a pioneer being scared of a beaver! Fancy a hero of the nation being afraid of a hedgehog! Marty was snoring peacefully. I laid my head on my pillow and it was cool and soft.

I must have dozed off, because I dreamed about Marty's injun coming out of the woods, with a tomahawk in his fist, saying over and over, "I don't say my prayers. I won't say my prayers!"

Suddenly I was wide-awake. I knew without opening my eyes that the tent had moved. Something had brushed against it! I felt the hair stand up on my head. I felt sweat leak out of my hands. A savage had surely come to murder Pa and steal Ma and Marty and me

away into slavery. He probably had a
bow, a whole bristle of arrows, a
hatchet, a knife and a pistol stolen from
a dead man.

If I called for help, Ma and Pa might
come running and get murdered. If I
didn't shout out, Marty and I might get
stolen away or scalped. Not that I had a
choice: my throat had closed up so tight
with fright that I could not make a
sound.

A great shadow
moved across
the tent – a
giant of a
shadow.

The fabric shuddered from end to end as the intruder brushed against it. Then it lurched wildly as the intruder trod on one of the guy ropes.

My heart lurched, too. I slid out of my sleeping roll and put it over Marty, so that he could not be seen. (He did not stir: Marty can sleep through anything.) What could I use for a weapon? I racked my brains. A shoe? Too small. The trout? Hardly. The bucket? On hands and knees, I crept towards the bucket. Just as I reached for it, there was a roar and a ripping, and a fist crammed with knives slashed its way clean through the canvas!

No, it was not a hand, but a paw, with claws as long as Bowie knives. And after the one paw, came the other, tearing the tent open wide enough for the head to follow.

A bear!

It thrust its face towards mine, black eyes a-glitter, black nostrils shining. A noise came from its throat so big that I heard it echo off Piano Ridge.

It knocked the bucket out of my hand, but the handle caught on its claws and, for a few seconds, it clanked the metal pail around its head, banging the tent pole, making the tent dance. The trout slithered down between us.

Then the bucket flew in my face, the bear stooped and snatched up the fish in its jaws, turned and lumbered off into the night. As it ran off, its fur was just a purple patch of dark against the glittering river.

Behind me, Marty sat up. "You covered me up! Perry, why d'you cover me up? I dreamed an injun was sitting on me! I'm all hot now!"

6

Music

The piano came today. The house is almost finished: no more sleeping in tents. So today our piano came jangling upriver from Cedar Falls in a barge. They nearly dropped it in the river, trying to get it ashore.

"Play something, Ma!" I said.

She shook her head. "It will need tuning before it can be played," she said.

But I could not wait for a piano tuner

to turn pioneer and move Out West and come to tune our piano.

"Play something, Ma. Please!"

So she sat down, right there on the riverbank, and played *Home Sweet Home*. The notes came out all flat and sharp, but I didn't care. I wondered if that old bear was listening up on Piano Ridge, hearing piano music for the first time.

"Better stop playing now," I said to Ma.

"I told you it would be out of tune," she said, closing the lid.

"Oh, it's not that," I said. "It's just that your music's so sweet... it might fetch down that bear again."

Part Two

The Savages of Bear Mountain

1

Changing Times

I know a pool on Bear Mountain where the trout watch the sky all day, then rise in the evening to sip flies off the surface. I like to go there when I have things to think through. I like to go there and sleep away the hottest part of the day. I have fired many an arrow into that pool, then followed it in, and fetched out a skewered trout for my brothers and me to eat.

There is one fish in there twice as big as all the rest and impossible to catch. I know: I've tried. Even the bears have never caught that trout, and they fish at Shining Pool more often than I do. I reckon it must be a spirit fish. So it's him I talk to when I have troubles, problems, things to think through.

My family has always spent their summers camped on the dawn side of Bear Mountain. I love it here. The bones of the mountain are as old as the world, and its trees older than my grandmother's grandmother. It is the place where my father is buried, and his father before him. Here there are as many spirits as there are trees, and when the wind blew, I used to think I could hear them speaking to me.

I don't hear them any more; not since the savages arrived.

At first the only white men on Bear Mountain were trappers, hunting in the woods, catching beaver down at the river. They were no different from us, The People.

But then the wagons began to arrive. The gangs of men on the wagons had no sooner arrived than they began killing trees. They cut the trunks through with great hatchets, yelping with joy as the crowns crashed down, spilling birds, spilling squirrels, spilling sappy blood. I used to watch from the neighbouring treetops, as they hacked off the branches and bark. Now the trees up there are too sparse to hide even a boy of my size. The savages have built a whole village of wooden buildings on Bear Mountain, so that they can spend all year cutting timber.

The smoke rises up, day and night, where they burn the leaves, burn the twigs, burn the nests and mosses and seedcases.

Sometimes I hear the Great Spirit groan and grieve, and then his tears splash down from the smoky sky and put out their fires. But why did the Great Spirit ever allow them to come here in the first place and build on the burial ground of The People? Does he have some terrible punishment in store for them? I hope so. I hate those tree-killers with a hate sharper and hotter than lightning.

My name is Man-of-the-Wet-Morning, though my brothers call me Dew. And if the Great Spirit won't drive the savages off Bear Mountain, I swear I'll do it for Him when I'm older.

41

2

The Need for a Gun

There is no fighting a man with a gun,
unless you have a gun yourself. When
the white man first came, he had the
guns and we did not. So we lost every
battle. We were pushed off our hunting
grounds. We were driven off our
summer pastures. When we fought back,
they shot us.

They don't seem to realize that the
Great Spirit gave this land to The People

when Time began, and meant us to stay here until the last day of the world. Once, a white man from the East came and offered to buy our land from us – as if land can be bought or sold! What? Did he think he was going to roll up the forests and plains and take them back with him on a wagon? We laughed and laughed at the idea.

We are not laughing any more.

When the loggers came to Bear Mountain, our father went to speak to them. He told them that the mountain was sacred and that the trees shaded the graves of our ancestors. They just took out their guns and threatened to shoot him if he did not get off their land. *Their* land! Ha! That's what white men do when they are afraid. They reach for their guns.

This summer, my father lies under

the shade of the mountain ash trees, beside Shining Pool where he taught us to fish. And the sawmill is built, and the trees are getting as thin as the hair on an old man's head.

White men are not to be trusted. Terrible stories come from far and wide, of the things they have done. In the south they are shooting the bison, just to starve the tribes of the Great Plains. They have a saying: "The only good injun is a dead injun." The word is a strange one, but we know what they mean by "injun": they mean The People. Us. How can you trust creatures who think like that?

Of course we trade with them. Sometimes, if a hunter sells enough skins to the trading post, he can afford to buy a rifle. That's what I've heard. That's what we want, my brothers and I.

"What do you need with a rifle, Dew?" says our sister Firefly. "One shot scares away every animal for miles around. One shot and your hunting is over for the day. Bow and arrows are stealthy. The old ways are the best."

"What do you know?" I tell her sternly. "What does a girl know about hunting? Stick to your weaving."

Firefly weaves blankets – wonderful blankets. Sometimes the threads tell stories in pictures, and she tells us the stories as she weaves. We have strictly forbidden her to get married until she has told us all the stories she knows. When this next blanket is finished, we will send her to the trading post with the others she has woven, to see if seven blankets will buy one rifle. My brother, Hot Embers says, "When people hate you, you need a weapon to defend yourself."

3

Berry Sickness

The trading post was crowded the day Firefly went there. Some new families had arrived from the East by wagon train. The store-man made Firefly stand aside until he had served them.

Then he refused to sell her a rifle. "No guns for injuns," he said. "I'll give you seven dollars for the blankets, but I don't sell guns to savages. Savages can't be trusted to use guns right."

Firefly did not know what to do. She was standing outside the trading post, with her blankets at her feet, when one of the men from the wagon train signalled that he wanted to trade with her. He was shivering with some kind of sickness and he wanted to get warm. His family must have been ill, too, because he wanted all seven blankets. Firefly showed, by miming, that she wanted a rifle in exchange, and the man gave her his rifle – just like that.

He gave her the sickness, too.

I've never seen a sickness like it. A few days after she got home, Firefly was covered all over in spots as red as the berries in the wood. She was hot and cold all at once, and her head ached. We brought the shaman to her, but he had never met this berry sickness before. His magic was powerless against it. He says she will die before the waning of the moon.

When I heard that, I felt a hole open up in my heart. I climbed to the top of Bear Mountain and prayed with all my might to the Great Sky Spirit to heal Firefly. But I think the noise and the smoke of the sawmill must have blinded and deafened Him. Or maybe He has moved off to another part of the sky, to get some peace and quiet.

The hole inside me just kept opening up, wider and wider, till it felt as if there were room for that big old Spirit Trout to swim through me. There is only one way to mend a hole like that. You have to stop it up.

Revenge is the only thing big enough.

4

Revenge

I went to Shining Pool and talked to
the Spirit Trout. I told him about
Firefly and the berry sickness. I told
him how I meant to kill a white man in
revenge for the harm they had done. I
showed him our new rifle, and I asked
him to help me.

As if by magic, a moment later, I
heard people coming up the path beside
the brook – clumsy, heavy-footed

people in boots. I knew at once they were settlers.

At once I hid myself in a hollow tree, on the edge of the wood, and who should come puffing up the path but Sawmill Man and two children! I have seen their encampment on the river bend: two tents and a buggy, two horses and a pile of timber from off the mountain. They are building themselves a hogan and a corral for the horses. How can they fence off a piece of ground, a million blades of grass, thirty trees, and say, "This is mine. I own it"? If I live to be older than my grandfather is, I shall never understand that. The earth belongs to the birds and the fish, the bears and The People, and to the Great Spirit who made us and put us here at the beginning of the world.

Hidden in the bushes, I cradled my

rifle close to my chest – the gun Firefly bought with her seven beautiful blankets. Through a knothole in the tree trunk, I had a perfect view of

Shining Pool. That is where Sawmill Man and his daughter stopped, set down their knapsacks, and began to fish. In *my* pool! They did not use a

bow and arrows, but sticks and string and flakes of bread. The little boy had not enough patience to fish. He just ran about, rowdy and disobedient, scaring all the fish away. What fools these white children are! My mother would have stopped up my mouth with leaves to silence me. In the end, Sawmill Man took the boy downstream and left him there.

I said to myself, "They think they can catch the Spirit Trout!" and it made me laugh under my breath. "They came here to catch fish, and instead I've caught them in my ambush!"

Here was the revenge I had been looking for. Here was a fitting target for my new rifle. I ducked out of my hollow tree, and wormed my way over rocks and dead logs, to a spot where I had a clear view of Sawmill Man. I laid

the rifle stock to my shoulder, the way I
have seen white men do. I took aim
along the barrel. Then I pulled the
trigger

CLICK.
Again I fired.
CLICK.

Breaking open the rifle, I felt the tears
push against the back of my eyes.

Firefly had bought us a gun, but she had bought us an *empty* gun. There were no bullets inside! With my bow and arrow I might have killed Sawmill Man where he sat dipping his bread bait in Shining Pool. Instead, I had brought a useless, empty gun.

I am half-grown. I have seen nine whole summers. Even so, I'm still too small to fight a grown white man with my bare hands. I bit my lip. I banged the flat of my hand against a rock, then I turned away in disgust.

Downstream, the little boy was throwing stones into the brook. In handfuls he picked them up and heaved them into the water. To and fro he ran, between the shade of a mountain ash and the riverbank, both hands full of stones. When I realized where he was playing, hate rolled around inside me like a clap of thunder. This was the spot we had chosen for our father's grave.

I thought of Firefly, dying of the white man's sickness.

I thought of my father, whose grave had been disturbed by this noisy brat.

I thought of those bison lying dead on the Great Plains.

I thought of the trees groaning as they fell, spilling their armfuls of birds' eggs.

I thought of my shame, in trying to shoot an enemy with an empty rifle.

I thought of Bear Mountain, mauled and plucked by these *outsiders*.

And I ran at the little boy, picked him up round his waist and flung him into the pool.

I thought he would sink out of sight, the water closing over his head. I thought the pool was much, much deeper. Fool that I am. When he spluttered and struggled to his feet, the water only came up to his waist. For a moment he just stared at me, eyes the size of full moons.

Then his mouth opened and I did not stay to hear how loud he could yell when he was really scared.

I took to my heels and ran. As I ran, I tried to scrape off my shame on the brambles and briars, but it clung to me. A fine warrior I had proved to be – attacking a little boy, because I couldn't fight his father!

Whole minutes later, I heard a gunshot ring out far behind me, but I don't think the bullet was aimed at me. In fact I don't think anyone came after me. I don't know why. I expected a great manhunt, with all the men from the sawmill scouring the wood for the wicked "injun" who had pushed the little boy into the brook. But no. Maybe you have to be a great man to merit a great manhunt - whereas I am just a little fool.

5

Gone

But do you know what? The next time I went back to Shining Pool, I found the Spirit Trout had gone. The huge brown one. The one I told all my hope and secrets to. Gone.

He must have left the pool to work his spirit magic over my sister. He *must* have done, because Firefly began to get better! Even though she had set one foot aboard Death's canoe, suddenly she stepped back ashore. Her fever went down. The berry-red rash faded and she started to get well. Who would have thought the spirits would take any notice of a little fool like me?

Firefly's eyes have not been good since her illness. She finds it difficult to weave her blankets. But she can still tell us stories. Sometimes she tells the story of the day the Spirit Trout swam down from Bear Mountain and into her dreams, and made her better, because I had asked it to come.

As soon as Firefly is strong enough, we shall leave Bear Mountain and spend the winter up-country. We don't have to stay here, season in, season out, like these white home-builders do. My sister and brothers and I will travel somewhere far away, where the trees have never seen a sawmill, where the trout have never seen a fishing rod, where the deer have never seen a pale pair of eyes. There must still be places like that. Somewhere.

Next summer, maybe I'll come back,

and burn down the sawmill or Sawmill Man's big wooden house at the bend in the river. There again, maybe I won't. When I told Firefly, she said, "Leave revenge to the Mountain. In spring, when the snows melt," she said, "all the little brooks turn into roaring cascades."

"I know that!"

"They pour into the big river, don't they, and swell it to twice its size? With all those trees cut down, the floods next year will be even worse, down by the sawmill and at the river bend."

For Firefly to be so wise, I think my Spirit Trout must still be swimming through her dreams.

About the author

I have written about 100 books – from fairy stories to adult novels. Ever since I was little, writing has helped me live my daydreams and escape my fearful shyness.

Every day, arriving home from junior school, I would put on my favourite fringed tunic, saddle up the garden wall (or Dad's motorbike), and ride off into the Wild West – sometimes a cowboy, more often an "injun". Hence this double-story.

Sadly, in real life, the "grand adventure" of the Pioneer Days brought little but tragedy to the native tribes of North America.